THE WAR IN AFGHANISTAN
12 THINGS TO KNOW

by Clara MacCarald

STORY
LIBRARY

www.12StoryLibrary.com

12-Story Library is an imprint of Peterson Publishing Company and Press Room Editions.

Produced for 12-Story Library by Red Line Editorial

Photographs ©: Anja Niedringhaus/AP Images, cover, 1; Gabriel-m/iStockphoto/Thinkstock, 4; Jim Collins/AP Images, 6; SFC Thomas R. Roberts, 7; Nicholas Kamm/AP Images, 8; US Department of Defense, 9, 10, 11, 13, 18, 19, 22, 23, 28, 29; Enric Marti/AP Images, 14; David Guttenfelder/AP Images, 15; Joe Raedle/AP Images, 16; US National Archives and Records Administration, 17; Staff Sgt. John Bainter/US Air Force, 20; Staff Sgt. Brian Ferguson/US Air Force, 21; Massoud Hossaini/AP Images, 24; Michael Ciaglo/The Colorado Springs Gazette/AP Images, 25; Patrick Tsui/FCO, 26; Najim Rahim/AP Images, 27

Content Consultant: Professor Brian Glyn Williams of University of Massachusetts-Dartmouth

Library of Congress Cataloging-in-Publication Data
Names: MacCarald, Clara, 1979- author.
Title: The War in Afghanistan : 12 things to know / by Clara MacCarald.
Other titles: War in Afghanistan twelve things to know
Description: Mankato, MN : 12-Story Library, [2017] | Series: America at war
  | Includes bibliographical references and index. | Audience: Grades 4-6.
Identifiers: LCCN 2016002429 (print) | LCCN 2016002588 (ebook) | ISBN
  9781632352682 (library bound : alk. paper) | ISBN 9781632353184 (pbk. :
  alk. paper) | ISBN 9781621434375 (hosted ebook)
Subjects: LCSH: Afghan War, 2001---Juvenile literature. | Taliban--Juvenile
  literature.
Classification: LCC DS371.412 .M24 2016 (print) | LCC DS371.412 (ebook) | DDC
  958.104/7--dc23
LC record available at http://lccn.loc.gov/2016002429

Printed in the United States of America
Mankato, MN
May, 2016

Access free, up-to-date content on this topic plus a full digital version of this book. Scan the QR code on page 31 or use your school's login at 12StoryLibrary.com.

Table of Contents

1

The Taliban Arises from Chaos

Since ancient times, people have fought for control of Afghanistan. Afghanistan's location makes it important for trade between people in the Middle East and Asia. One war began in 1978. A new, Communist government had taken control of the country. Many people did not like the new government. Uprisings took place in the eastern part of the country.

By 1979, Afghanistan was in a civil war. The Soviet Union was also Communist. It entered the war to help the Afghan government. Other nations, such as the United States, helped the rebels resist the Soviets. A wealthy Saudi man named Osama bin Laden also sent money to help the rebels. He even went to Afghanistan to take part in the fight and train other fighters.

Afghanistan is rugged. It is about the size of Texas.

In 1988, bin Laden was in Afghanistan to help with the war effort. He started a group called al-Qaeda in nearby Pakistan. Through al-Qaeda, bin Laden dreamed of spreading the jihad, or struggle to be better followers of Islam, from Afghanistan. But the group wanted to support new jihads in other countries. Al-Qaeda decided they would leave Afghanistan when the Soviets did. The Soviets left in 1989, and so did bin Laden. But the Afghans were still fighting each other in a civil war.

Bin Laden returned to Saudi Arabia. There, he was seen as a war hero. But that changed when he began calling the Saudi king un-Islamic for letting US troops into Saudi Arabia to fight against Iraq. Bin Laden was forced out of the country. He went to live in Sudan.

In the meantime, a group called the Taliban appeared in Afghanistan in 1994. They fought for the country and took control of most of it by 1996. The Taliban promised peace, but they ruled with an iron fist. They followed a strict form of Islam. Their beliefs led them to ban music and

252,000
Size, in square miles (652,677 sq km), of Afghanistan.

- People have fought over Afghanistan for hundreds of years.
- From 1979 to 1989, troops from the Soviet Union fought in Afghanistan.
- The Taliban controlled the country by 1996.
- Al-Qaeda leader Osama bin Laden returned to Afghanistan around 1996.
- The Taliban supported al-Qaeda.

movies. They punished crimes in cruel ways. They kept all women from going to school or working. Groups resisting the Taliban formed the Northern Alliance.

Around the same time, Sudan threw bin Laden out. The United States had accused the Sudanese government of supporting terrorism. Bin Laden returned to Afghanistan. This time he helped the Taliban. In return, the Taliban supported him and al-Qaeda. Al-Qaeda had big plans in the works.

9/11 Leads to War

September 11, 2001, began with calm skies over New York City. That changed just before 9:00 a.m. A plane crashed into one of the Twin Towers of the World Trade Center. People thought it was an accident. But then, a second plane hit the center's other tower. Both towers fell. Another plane crashed into the Pentagon in Washington, DC. The Pentagon is the headquarters of the United States military. A fourth plane crashed into a field in Pennsylvania.

More than 400 police officers and firefighters died in the September 11, 2001, terrorist attacks.

Terrorists from al-Qaeda had taken over the planes. The events that took place that day shocked the United States. People around the world extended sympathy to Americans. Citizens from more

THINK ABOUT IT

Following 9/11, many countries agreed to help the United States with the war on terrorism. In what ways did they help, and why?

On September 14, 2001, President Bush used a bullhorn to speak to rescue workers from atop the rubble at the site of the crumbled World Trade Center.

than 80 countries died in the attacks. People called the attacks 9/11 because they happened on September 11.

President George Bush called the attacks "acts of war." The United States told the Taliban to hand over bin Laden and other members of al-Qaeda. When the Taliban refused, the US government prepared for war.

Bush announced there would be a war on terrorism itself. It was not against Islam. The United States asked other countries for help. They built a coalition. Some countries offered routes to Afghanistan. Others offered troops. Bush warned the Taliban that time was running out.

2,973
Number of people who lost their lives in the 9/11 attacks.

- Al-Qaeda attacked the United States on September 11, 2001.
- The United States told the Taliban to hand over members of al-Qaeda.
- When the Taliban refused, the United States prepared for war.

Operation Enduring Freedom Begins

On the night of October 7, 2001, a huge ship floated in the Arabian Sea. It shook as a plane took off from its deck. The bomber plane was headed for Afghanistan, hundreds of miles away. The war in Afghanistan had begun. The United States called it Operation Enduring Freedom. Bombers flew from as far away as the state of Missouri. The planes bombed al-Qaeda camps. They struck the Taliban's military sites.

The coalition built by the United States had two big goals. They wanted to destroy al-Qaeda. They also wanted to bring down the Taliban. The Taliban had protected bin Laden even after 9/11. What the coalition did not want to do was occupy Afghanistan. They wanted other Afghans to take over the nation.

Assault ship USS *Peleliu* sails in the Arabian Sea in support of Operation Enduring Freedom in 2001.

Northern Alliance troops at Bagram Air Base, the largest US military air base in Afghanistan

The coalition partnered with the Northern Alliance, which had long opposed the Taliban. Before the war, the alliance was not strong enough to overthrow the Taliban. But now, small teams of US soldiers fought on the ground alongside these Afghan forces. The teams could help organize local fighters. And they could call in bombers.

34,400
Number of packets of food and medicine dropped the first night of bombing during Operation Enduring Freedom.

- Operation Enduring Freedom began with bombing on October 7, 2001.
- The coalition wanted to destroy al-Qaeda.
- They also wanted to bring down the Taliban.
- The Northern Alliance and the coalition began working together.
- The coalition fought in the air and on the ground.

A PUBLIC RELATIONS WAR

The coalition wanted Afghans to support the war. They tried to limit civilian deaths and provide humanitarian aid. Planes dropped supplies, as well as bombs, over Afghanistan. Later, they dropped explanations of the war. Leaflets said the attacks were aimed at the Taliban. They were not against the people of Afghanistan or Islam. Almost all Afghans are Muslims. US planes dropped radios preset to a station that also explained the purpose of the war.

Kandahar Falls, Bringing Down the Taliban

After a slow start, the Northern Alliance swept across the northern parts of Afghanistan. They had fewer fighters than the Taliban, but now they had coalition support. The coalition dropped supplies for the alliance. When the Taliban fought back, the coalition bombed them. The Taliban learned to take cover.

The alliance approached the nation's capital, Kabul. Civilians welcomed them. The Taliban tried to defend the city, but they were weak from air strikes. Shortly after the attack began, the Taliban fled. The combination of ground and air forces had broken their spirit. The alliance entered the city on November 13, 2001. There was chaos but also joy. People celebrated their freedom from the Taliban. Music played in the streets for the first time in years.

Some US soldiers joined with the Northern Alliance to fight.

The coalition took control of the skies over Afghanistan in late 2001.

The coalition looked for allies in the southern and eastern parts of the country. The Taliban still held a big Afghan city. It was called Kandahar. The coalition's southern allies advanced. They expected resistance. Instead, the city fell without much of a fight on December 7. The Taliban lost control of Zabul Province two days later, on December 9. It was their last remaining stronghold in Afghanistan. Their rule had ended. The coalition was surprised at how fast the Taliban had fallen.

THINK ABOUT IT

The Taliban banned many things. How would your life be different if playing cards, music, and movies were forbidden? Would you risk being punished to have those things?

5
Number of years the Taliban ruled Afghanistan.

- The Northern Alliance swept across the country.
- The capital fell on November 13, 2001.
- Taliban rule ended on December 9, 2001.

11

Bonn Agreement Shows a Way Forward

As Taliban rule crumbled, the war neared one of its goals. Now, Afghanistan needed new leaders. But different ethnic groups of Afghans were in conflict. They had different ideas about how the nation should be ruled. The United Nations (UN) chose a neutral place for them to meet. On November 27, 2001, more than two dozen leaders from four Afghan groups met in Bonn, Germany. They created a new government. Four of the Afghan leaders were women. Women had been shut out of public life under the Taliban. But they would be a part of planning the future.

The Afghans argued. Some ethnic groups distrusted each other because of a history of rivalry. Finally, on December 5, they signed an agreement. They chose a man named Hamid Karzai to lead a temporary government starting on December 22. Karzai was part of the ethnic group called the Pashtuns. Afghans felt a Pashtun leader might be acceptable to the Pashtun majority in the country. Two women were given roles in the government. The agreement

THE ROLE OF NATO

The United States is part of the North Atlantic Treaty Organization (NATO). Twenty-eight countries belong to NATO. It is a group of allies. They have promised to defend each other from attacks. After 9/11, NATO countries agreed to support the war against the Taliban. NATO led the International Security Assistance Force (ISAF) beginning on August 11, 2003. At times, ISAF has had more than 130,000 troops. They helped rebuild Afghanistan and also fought for peace.

requested support from other nations to rebuild Afghanistan. It asked the United Nations to help prepare for an election.

The Afghans wanted to provide their own security for the country. They knew they would need to build an army and a police force. The process would take time. Until then, they asked the United Nations for troops to help keep the peace. These troops would become known as the International Security Assistance Force (ISAF).

27
Number of Afghans who took part in the Bonn talks.

- Afghanistan needed new leaders once the Taliban was gone.
- Afghans met in Bonn, Germany, on November 27, 2001.
- On December 5, they agreed to a temporary government led by Hamid Karzai.
- They asked for help from other countries.

On December 20, 2001, the UN authorized ISAF's creation. Eighteen countries took part, including the United States.

6

Battle of Tora Bora Misses bin Laden

The Taliban and al-Qaeda were on the run in early December 2001. The United States did not want bin Laden to get away. He and his group were responsible for 9/11. Destroying al-Qaeda was an aim of the war. Many members of al-Qaeda fled to Tora Bora. Bin Laden was one of them.

Tora Bora is a valley among steep mountains. It is close to Pakistan. During the Soviet invasion, Afghans used a system of tunnels in the area. The tunnels were carved thousands of feet into the mountains. Al-Qaeda used them as a training center and for shelter. They stored many weapons in the tunnels.

Eastern Alliance forces searched Tora Bora for Taliban members.

Underground, al-Qaeda fighters were safer from coalition bombs.

The coalition bombed Tora Bora cave entrances. Explosions caused rockslides in the mountains. Al-Qaeda fought back. Afghans hired by the United States led the ground assault. But storming the caves was dangerous. The Afghans hesitated to do it. The coalition tried to keep al-Qaeda fighters from escaping to Pakistan. Still most fighters slipped away, including bin Laden.

Sometimes, rival groups of Afghans who were attempting to destroy al-Qaeda shot at each other instead of at the enemy.

9
Distance, in miles (14 km), to Pakistan from Tora Bora.

- Al-Qaeda fighters fled to Tora Bora.
- Tora Bora had vast tunnels for hiding.
- The coalition attacked.
- Bin Laden escaped the fighting.

NEIGHBORING COUNTRIES

Afghanistan and Pakistan are neighbors. Pakistan was one of the only countries that accepted the Taliban when they were in charge. Later, Pakistan agreed to help the coalition. The Taliban found refuge in Pakistan anyway. The Pakistani government exercised little control along the border of the two countries. Many people there had ties with the Taliban.

Operation Anaconda Squeezes Taliban

In 2002, it seemed the war might soon be over. But the new Afghan government faced an old danger. Members of al-Qaeda and the Taliban had survived coalition attacks. They hid in the mountains of southeastern Afghanistan and in Pakistan. Their fighters began to amass in Shah-e-Kot Valley. Shah-e-Kot is near Tora Bora. The coalition planned to challenge them. The mission would be called Operation Anaconda.

For the first time, US forces were a big part of the ground fight. The plan was to attack the valley. US and Afghan troops would secure the mountain passes. They would block enemies trying to flee. The assault began on March 2. Three villages lay in the valley. Their inhabitants

Operation Anaconda was the largest battle US troops faced in Afghanistan.

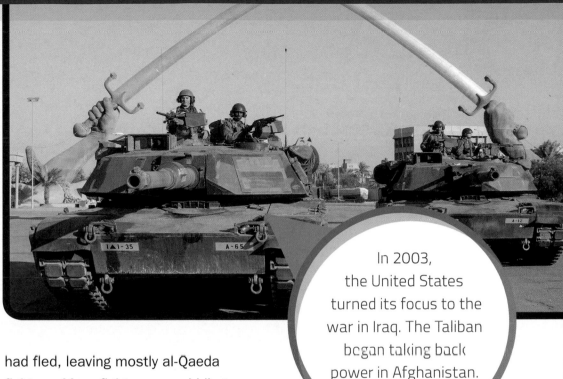

In 2003, the United States turned its focus to the war in Iraq. The Taliban began taking back power in Afghanistan.

had fled, leaving mostly al-Qaeda fighters. More fighters were hiding in Shah-e-Kot than the coalition expected.

Some coalition troops found themselves under heavy fire. Bad weather slowed others down as they fought toward their positions. The fierce battle lasted for days. In the end, US troops were successful. The coalition controlled the valley by March 12. Fighting ended a week later. The allies disagreed about the results. The United States claimed only a few men from al-Qaeda and the Taliban escaped. Al-Qaeda claimed hundreds may have gotten out alive.

7
Number of countries involved in combat in Operation Anaconda.

- Enemy fighters amassed in Shah-e-Kot Valley in early 2002.
- They posed a danger to the new Afghan government.
- Operation Anaconda aimed to destroy them.
- Some members of the Taliban and al-Qaeda escaped.

Taliban Fights Back with IEDs

The first elections of the new Afghan government were held on October 9, 2004. The people elected Hamid Karzai to remain as president. People's lives had improved. Roads and buildings had been rebuilt. Children were vaccinated. Girls were going back to school.

Yet Afghanistan was still not stable. Not everyone supported the government. Afghans were angry that coalition strikes on the Taliban had killed civilians. Some Afghan officials were dishonest. Many people were still very poor. Farmers were tempted to make money by growing poppy flowers, which are used to make an illegal drug called opium.

The Taliban and their allies moved freely in some parts of Afghanistan, such as Helmand Province in the south. Other Taliban and al-Qaeda fighters staying in Pakistan crossed into Afghanistan to attack and then returned to safety in Pakistan. The Taliban wanted to topple the new Afghan government. Taliban fighters launched bombs and rockets at military bases. They attacked Afghan civilians and troops. They targeted unarmed aid workers and government employees.

In 2004 and 2005, Taliban fighters began making more improvised explosive

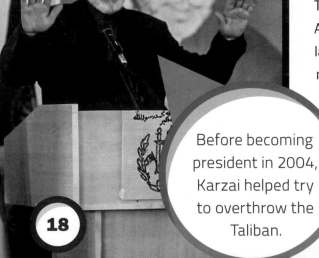

Before becoming president in 2004, Karzai helped try to overthrow the Taliban.

devices (IEDs). IEDs are homemade bombs. Most IEDs are set off when a person detonates a trip wire, pressure plate, or remote control. But some use timers.

Taliban fighters used IEDs to attack the coalition from a distance. IEDs could be placed beside roads or paths. Sometimes, they were left in houses soldiers might search. For greater safety, coalition soldiers drove armored trucks. The armor could lessen a blast. IEDs also struck civilians.

US troops train how to properly mark the location of IEDs.

50

Approximate number of attacks made by the Taliban and its allies per month in much of 2005.

- Afghanistan held an election on October 9, 2004.
- Hamid Karzai was now the elected president.
- The Taliban attacked troops and civilians.
- They increased their use of homemade bombs.

SOLDIERS AID AFGHANS

US soldiers fought with the Northern Alliance, but they also helped civilians. They assisted the villages of Mollai in 2006. Soldiers handed out food, clothes, and school supplies. They helped villagers build schools. One school taught girls. The Taliban had kept girls out of school. Anti-government fighters still opposed girls' schools. They attacked students and teachers. But locals welcomed the girls' school in Mollai.

Drones Reduce Risks to Soldiers

Armed drones were used in Afghanistan starting on the first night of Operation Enduring Freedom. A drone is a plane controlled remotely by someone on the ground. Drones are appealing to armies because they can be used to spy on people and targets. There is no crew who can be injured if the drone is shot down.

Modern drones have video cameras. They can act like scouts to help prepare for military operations, such as Anaconda. In Afghanistan, they spied on enemy fighters. Many drones were used to kill individual terrorists. Some even had missiles that were used to kill rebel groups.

THINK ABOUT IT

Many Americans disagree with the military using drones, especially on bombing missions. Why do you think this is? Do you agree or disagree?

The MQ-9 Reaper is a remotely piloted aircraft.

In 2008, drone strikes greatly increased in the parts of Pakistan where the Taliban was hiding. Drones could fly over remote areas and use cameras to spy on the Taliban. They could follow the Taliban into Pakistan and kill them inside their mountain hideout. Many Pakistanis were upset by drones operating in their country.

Drones can stay in the air for a long time.

11
Number of countries with armed drones as of 2013.

- Drones are planes controlled from the ground.
- They have been used in Afghanistan since the start of Operation Enduring Freedom.
- Some drones spied on the enemy to help prepare for war.
- Drone strikes in Afghanistan increased in 2008.

EARLY US DRONES

The United States has used drones in several wars. Unmanned planes carried bombs in World War II. Drones took photos during the Vietnam War. A drone even observed bin Laden in 2000, a year before 9/11. Although the United States knew where he was, they were unable to confront him. Soldiers could not get to his location in time. The drone itself had no weapons. The military's frustration led to new, armed drones.

Troops Surge to Subdue Taliban

In 2009, President Barack Obama took office. The Taliban gained strength because most US troops had been sent to fight in Iraq. Obama needed to reduce the Taliban's power before the United States could leave Afghanistan. He approved a plan to send thousands of new troops to Afghanistan in 2010. The surge of troops could push back the Taliban from the lands they had conquered. Obama hoped to begin bringing the new troops home in less than two years.

The first task was to take Marja. At the time, Marja was the headquarters of the Taliban in Afghanistan. The area supported the Taliban with money from the production of illegal drugs.

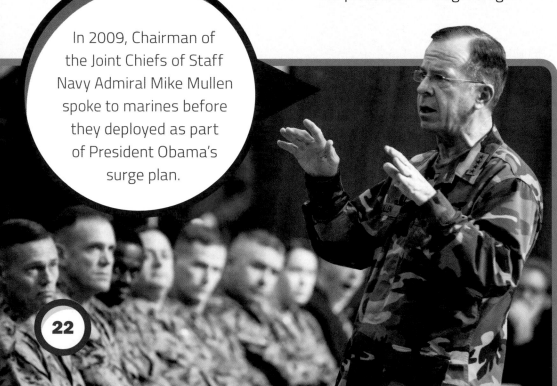

In 2009, Chairman of the Joint Chiefs of Staff Navy Admiral Mike Mullen spoke to marines before they deployed as part of President Obama's surge plan.

Troops rest while clearing a compound in Helmand in 2010.

The United States warned the Taliban to leave Marja. It wanted to limit fighting to reduce civilian deaths. Marines were flown into the center of Marja on February 13, 2010. They attacked the Taliban from all directions. IEDs were everywhere. After a short fight, the Taliban gave up.

The surge troops continued to fight throughout the south. They took control of areas such as the Helmand and Kandahar Provinces. Troops engaged local Afghans. They helped with construction and government. The surge troops left in September 2012. Afghan forces stayed in the southern provinces to secure the gains the United States had made. But some Afghans worried their own troops could not keep the peace. They lacked discipline and a powerful air force.

33,000
Number of US troops added during the surge.

- President Obama wanted to turn the tide against the Taliban.
- In 2010, Obama sent extra troops to Afghanistan.
- The surge troops first took Marja.
- When the surge troops left in 2012, Afghans took over.

23

US Combat Mission Ends

The war was expensive for the United States. Many lives were lost. Almost 10,000 civilians were killed just in 2014. Approximately 5,000 Afghan troops died. Although the fighting continued, the United States was tired of war. Bin Laden, a main target of the war, had been killed in Pakistan on May 2, 2011.

On December 28, 2014, ISAF held a service at its headquarters in Kabul. People from many countries were in the audience. The green and white ISAF flag flying over the headquarters was lowered. A general rolled it up. The war in Afghanistan was officially over. The Afghan military now took the lead. US President Obama was not present at the event, but he spoke about it. He said the war had disrupted terrorism and helped Afghans.

Afghanistan now had more than 350,000 of its own troops. But the world did not abandon Afghanistan completely. The general who folded the ISAF flag unfurled a new one. This flag represented Operation Resolute Support, a new international mission led

Lieutenant General Joseph Anderson, left, folded the ISAF flag on December 28, 2014.

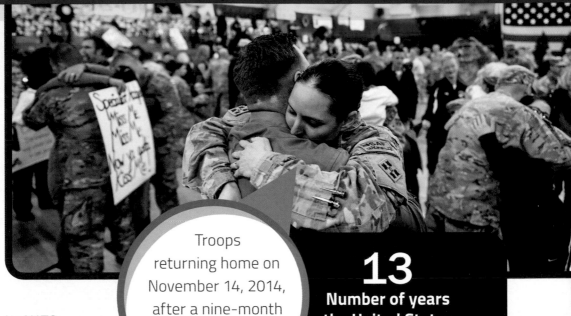

Troops returning home on November 14, 2014, after a nine-month deployment to Afghanistan

by NATO. The United States also began Operation Freedom's Sentinel on January 1, 2015. As part of this operation, nearly 10,000 US troops stayed behind. The focus of the two new missions would be training and supporting Afghan forces.

13

Number of years the United States fought in Operation Enduring Freedom.

- The war ended on December 28, 2014.
- Afghan forces took over the fight against the Taliban.
- A smaller mission started at the same time to keep supporting the Afghans.

THE COST OF WAR

Operation Enduring Freedom was the longest war the United States ever fought. It cost approximately $1 trillion. There was also a human cost. The war had many casualties. The coalition had approximately 3,500 deaths. According to the US Department of Defense, this included 2,355 Americans. An additional 20,071 US troops were wounded in action. Afghanistan suffered thousands of casualties as well.

Violence Endures after the War

Afghans hoped new leadership would bring order to the country. They elected a new president, Ashraf Ghani, three months before the official end of the war in 2014. But the country remained poor and dangerous. The Taliban returned to areas where they had been removed by the surge.

The Taliban and other armed groups continued to fight. They were supported by drug money. Even Afghan forces sometimes threatened or killed civilians for money or while fighting. Thousands of Afghans fled their war-torn country.

On September 28, 2015, the Taliban overran Kunduz City, a provincial capital. It was their biggest victory since 2001. The Taliban withdrew from the city after 15 days of fighting with Afghan and US forces.

Afghan President Ashraf Ghani served as finance minister from 2002 to 2004.

London Conference on Afghanistan

During the battle, US bombs accidentally hit a hospital. Thirty people died. The world was horrified. But Afghan politicians were less critical. They were afraid of speaking out against the United States because they wanted US troops to stay.

President Obama had vowed to bring all US troops home by the end of 2016. But on October 15, 2015, Obama announced a change of plans. He said thousands of US troops would stay in Afghanistan through 2017 or longer. The Taliban and al-Qaeda were no longer the only threats in the area. The United States also was concerned about a new terrorist group called the Islamic State of Iraq and Syria (ISIS). It followed a harsh version of Islam and was taking over parts of Syria and Iraq. US troops continued to train and support Afghan forces in their fight against these groups. Time will tell if they can help bring stability to Afghanistan.

President Obama apologized after the US military bombed a hospital in Kunduz City.

9,800
Number of US troops still in Afghanistan as of 2015.

- New conflicts arose in Afghanistan after the war ended.
- The Taliban was still a threat in many parts of the country.
- The Taliban captured Kunduz City on September 28, 2015, but left 15 days later.
- On October 15, President Obama announced US troops would stay until at least 2017.

12 Key Dates

September 11, 2001
Al-Qaeda attacks the United States with planes, hitting the World Trade Center and the Pentagon.

October 7, 2001
Operation Enduring Freedom begins with bombs dropped across Afghanistan.

November 13, 2001
The Northern Alliance enters Kabul, the capital of Afghanistan.

December 5, 2001
Afghan leaders sign an agreement creating the nation's new temporary government.

December 9, 2001
The Taliban loses control of Afghanistan.

December 22, 2001
A new, temporary government led by Hamid Karzai takes power.

March 2, 2002
Operation Anaconda attacks Taliban forces gathering in a valley.

October 9, 2004
Afghanistan holds its first elections, with Hamid Karzai keeping the presidency.

February 13, 2010
Extra troops from the surge attack Marja, a Taliban stronghold.

May 2, 2011
US troops kill Osama bin Laden in Pakistan.

December 28, 2014
The war officially ends with a ceremony in Kabul.

January 1, 2015
The United States begins Operation Freedom's Sentinel to support Afghan forces.

Glossary

allies
People or groups who support each other.

casualty
A person who has been killed or injured.

civilian
A person who is not part of an armed group.

coalition
A group of allies working together.

ethnic
Relating to people sharing ties through birth and culture.

humanitarian
Involved in efforts to make other people's lives better.

Islam
A religion that began in Arabia and is now the second largest in the world.

jihad
For most Muslims, a peaceful struggle to be better followers of Islam; some Muslims, such as al-Qaeda, take an extreme view, committing violent acts against non-Islamic countries.

Muslim
A follower of Islam.

operation
A military action.

rebels
People who rise up against the government or ruler.

terrorism
The use of violence or threats to pursue political goals.

terrorist
A person who uses or calls for terrorism.

For More Information

Books

Englar, Mary. *September 11.* Mankato, MN: Compass Point Books, 2006.

Nardo, Don. *Understanding Afghanistan Today.* Hockessin, DE: Mitchell Lane, 2014.

Souter, Janet, and Gerry Souter. *War in Afghanistan and Iraq: The Daily Life of the Men and Women Serving in Afghanistan and Iraq.* London: Carlton Books, 2011.

Visit 12StoryLibrary.com

Scan the code or use your school's login at **12StoryLibrary.com** for recent updates about this topic and a full digital version of this book. Enjoy free access to:

- Digital ebook
- Breaking news updates
- Live content feeds
- Videos, interactive maps, and graphics
- Additional web resources

Note to educators: Visit 12StoryLibrary.com/register to sign up for free premium website access. Enjoy live content plus a full digital version of every 12-Story Library book you own for every student at your school.

31

Index

About the Author

Clara MacCarald is a writer from central New York with a master's degree in biology. She has written many articles about science and local news for community newspapers.

READ MORE FROM 12-STORY LIBRARY

Every 12-Story Library book is available in many formats. For more information, visit 12StoryLibrary.com.